Experiment A
What should a God want?

HOOMAN

Copyright © 2025 Hoomex Pty Ltd
All rights reserved.
ISBN 978-0-9756474-3-1

DEDICATION
dedicated to hope.

Experiment A

Before you begin:

This book is the second in the series of Hooman Experiments and follows Experiment F: Are you a good human being?

It is suggested that these books be read in order.

The conditions for this experiment are the same for the whole series and the most critical ones are these:

• You are the subject in solitude.
• You know everything that you have known till now.
• I will not refer to any faith or reference any other man or woman.
• You have been removed from the society and can no longer contact anyone until the end of this experiment.
• You will read each line and not skip.
• Be orderly and understand the previous step before reading any further as the entire experiment is a single chain of event.

Experiment A

Now, ready?

CONTENTS

The Need	3
The Problem Defined	3
The Issue	3
The Management Framework	8
The Problem with Humans	8
The One and Only	23
Duality Loop	24
Revealing Face vs Attribute	36
The Time of Creation	41
One or Two	42
The Problem of Two	47
Hierarchy, Equality or Differentiation	55
The Creation of Many	69
Assignment of Identity	70
Inevitable Differentiation	73
Freedom	76
Imagination	83
The Method of Speech	90
The Start	94
The End	99
The Why	104

The Protection of Word	110
Avoid Human Pollution	119
The Timeframe	127
The End and Beyond	133
The End	133
The Beyond	133

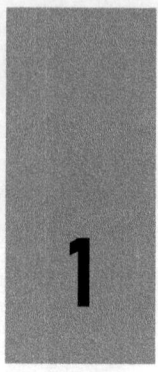# The Need

The Problem Defined

What should a God want?

The Issue

In our first experiment F, we realized that Humans are a minority on this earth. People are everywhere. People are those beings that belong to the humankind but have yet to realize that once they classify themselves as Human, they are implicitly acknowledging the following:

1. The existence of God
2. The existence of pain.
3. The absence of any viable alternate to the story of creation.

The level above humans contains all those beings that are just people, as they are not ready or willing to classify themselves as a human being and wish to be known by some other generic or specific titles, because they have that choice, just like you.

However, once any person affirms their status as a Human, they need a game plan to manage this combined human and being existence.

Let us assume that for now on, you have also labeled yourself as a human being to begin this experiment. You can of course opt out of this label, any time during or after the end of this experiment.

So, you need a game plan to manage your human being existence, right?

Experiment A   The Need

Explanation:

You could read being and nothingness, phenomenology of spirit or other similar easy-to-read works, but I will stick to my promise that I will not make you read anything.

For my younger readers, and I sure hope there are none, these two are hundreds of pages each of philosophy masterpieces that are supposed to tell you something but only if you have read their critiques. Studying them would mean relying on other humans, no matter how mega super deluxe brainiac they might have been. Even if your chosen human has the brain of three people combined, I have a simple right to say words like who, what and why. Don't trust that person, etc. and so on. Let us avoid a fight here, shall we? This series is just about you in solitude and peace.

Therefore, all published works will never be referred to anywhere in this experiment as well, exactly like we did for the first Experiment F.

Besides, Humans do not need knowledge to understand anything.

Detour:
If what you are trying to understand has already been understood by another human, you are just ignorant about it. You are ignorant about so many 'its' that it is impossible to list them all.

Therefore, it makes no sense for you to try to imagine your own ignorance. If something exists, which you are ignorant about and irrespective of whether another human knows about it or not, the tool of knowledge could be one way to discover the meaning of whatever 'it' is.

Experiment A   The Need

This is not the way we experiment. This is the knowledge free method.

(Trust me, this way is easier for lazy people like us.)

2 The Management Framework

The Problem with Humans

I am sorry for all the detours and explanations. I just wanted to revise the lab conditions of our experimental world.

So where were we. Ahh……yes! I just remembered that we are trying to answer a simple question titled: What should a God want?

Now towards the end of our previous Experiment F, I had asked whether you were also someone that has agreed to call yourself a human being.

If you had answered yes, this confirmation would have provided me with the right to 'assume' that you are also 'confirming' the existence of God and your choice to believe in one or another. Right?

Yes, No, Maybe?

Yes, you could still say that you do belong to the humankind but are not sure about this whole 'God' thing that I keep referring to.

So, let us breakdown what we know by now for sure.

The only thing that we have established is that no matter who you are, you can be grouped to one of these kinds of people:

1. A human being or that sort of person

2. Free bird 2000, made from strawberries, or

3. Some fluke.

Every person in all these kinds has choice.

I am aware which group most of my readers belong to, and yes, all birds should be free.

Group 1 is where I belong and that is why I know that whenever any other person is mentioned, I must acknowledge their choice.

Just like you have a choice right now: to continue or not to continue, to laugh or to cry, to stop reading, all these choices are yours to make at your own free will.

At this moment, you are the only reality which you can ever confirm. It is just you and your choice, which are the only two certainties that you can be aware and in control of in this experimental world of ours.

Like I have mentioned previously, since I am a human who acknowledges that I have a choice to believe in God, and I do. However, you may not.

That is the highest level of difference that can exist between all people that you see around you.

Which brings us to Aliens… Although we really ought to write a separate series for them. For now, let us say that you may or may not call yourself a human being, but you still have the choice.

What drives your choice? How do you choose what to do? Is it because you desire something?

That is the problem with being a human being.
We desire.

The Desire for Nothing

Welcome back. So, what do you desire?

1.   Nothing?

2.   Something?

3. Everything?

Really lazy people will truly appreciate the senselessly brutal approach I have taken towards all human desires and basically put them in 3 easy to understand buckets and have also been kind enough to put numbers just before them so you would not need to count.

Do you like to count?

If you said yes, you just stated your personal liking towards something. Same thing if you said no.

The answer above was your choice and the first thing that you need to question is if anyone else can take away this choice of yours?

What if you were left uneducated because of poverty? What if your dog ate all your books? What if you were not allowed to study a conceptual subject by your parents? What if someone locked you in a room that left you unable to attend any Maths class? What if you cannot see or hear and have never seen a number or word in your life?

The questions above might have made you think that there are many different types of people and there are certain groups and subgroups that may respond to any question about anything, like enjoying Maths, in any manner they choose.

Imagining all these people, can you, yourself, take away the right of choice from any other person?

Once again, you could lock them and not let them vote for instance, turn them deaf so that they cannot hear, torture them to blindness but the human's choice would still exist and at many levels, for example:

thoughts, actions, and words.

Not all of them can ever be removed permanently by any person from any other person. That is the first right granted to you as inhabitant of this earth.

The un-stealable right to choose, based on whatever you desire at any time, for as long as you are alive.

If you are still alive and have any need related to either your human or your being, you have no option but to acknowledge that during your entire lifetime, you can only desire something.

Which brings us back to the other two buckets that are nothing and everything.

All people have a problem, that everyone of us desires something. Also, we saw that there is a limitation that none of us can stop others from desiring.

When you desire ice cream, you must refuse milk, sugar, fruit, and ice, all of which you could have consumed by itself, but you would rather have some other people mix those ingredients all up into a sweet creamy cold treat, someone else to pack it up and another to wait for you to come buy it. Why?

Because ice cream is what you desire, it is your choice, your preference, your right.

Therefore, you just chose something and rejected something else. Because we can only desire something, we can never truly desire everything.

Which leaves us with just one option. The desire for nothing.

Now, if I asked you to desire nothing, you would probably die, if you are still alive. Simply, for as long as you are a human with a being attached, you must constantly desire something or else your being will cease leaving your human homeless.

As your human is non-physical, your human desires need your being to materialise.

For instance, for you to read the next lines, you must now make a conscious decision within your brain, or any other organ of your anatomy, where your inner human thinks, and decide if you want to read it or not, before asking your body's controlling nerves to direct your eyes to move onto the next line.

Ahh… you desired it as you chose to read further.

Up till this point in the experiment, all we have really established is that you have a problem of desires that is just yours and will never finish as long as you live or want to eat.

It is time to discard two options and declare that you do not desire everything and nothing.

In our experimental world now, there is only you and your desires as known realities.

The next reality we can also confirm is nature. Introduction to nature is necessary at this stage to ensure that we can imagine a place where two certainties, you and your choice can exist, and nature is also what is going to define how these two and other so far undiscovered realities will generate, and how they will all be linked to each other.

If you wanted to know more about this nature that you know as of now, within which you and your desires exist, you must complete the following equation:

Everything in nature = Beings that desire + Anything that does not.

As we belong in the first part of this equation, we need to think if there is anyone else after the plus. Therefore, our primary question can now be easily rephrased into this:

Is there an entity in nature that desires nothing? What if you desire to search for One that does not desire?

What could that be?

If you got the ability to create another certainty within this nature that interacts with you but does not desire like humans, how would it exist?

Would it be smaller than you and dependent on you?

That would not work because it would desire you. Therefore, if humans ever want to interact with someone that does not desire like them, they must stumble upon the concept of a certainty higher, stronger, smarter and beyond their imagination.

Primarily, our inability to find someone who has no desire is the source of all quests for a Creator in our entire history. We have not discovered a single being thus far, that can survive on its own. Do you know any form of life that can exist without something else?

Even the dead earth needs sunlight to produce strawberries that you needed for someone to make your ice cream or even for our Free Bird 2000 model. This is the cycle of dependence that we can observe in everything that we know and cannot break free from.

This cycle of dependence is the inherent driver of our desires that translates into your choices which can either cause you pain or joy.

What if we searched for someone independent, who does not need or desire anything? Only that entity can potentially be the Creator that pushed all this in motion.

The One that desires nothing that we can imagine.

The One where our duality finishes.

That is the concept of Singularity.

3   The One and Only

Do you think that Human beings need a Creator?

The human problem described previously led us to a point where we desired a singularity to complete our equation about nature.

Therefore, for a higher entity to exist as singularity, we should perhaps start to imagine the question number one.

One?

Yes, that is the first natural question. If we are to assume an entity as creator, can there be only One or do we need more?

Experiment A   The One and Only

Duality Loop

Have you decided that your human existence requires a Creator?

If no, let us see what the competing story says.

If yes, your first problem is to imagine a singularity in any shape or form that you desire. For instance, you could say that your assumed God is named XYZ123 but that is not the point.

The point is who created XYZ123?

This is normally the first question that gets asked whenever any person imagines an all-powerful entity that does not desire anything.

This is called the duality loop. There are many ways this question or paradox can be approached.

If I can create and I am created, the creator must also be created, is the simplest form of the loop of duality.

If I am created and can observe duality within, so must the creator be a duality, if the creator is also created.

For your creator to be a singularity, this loop of duality must close.

Primarily there are two possibilities that will

Experiment A   The One and Only

___

keep this loop open.

First, if we have multiple creators with their own domains:

If your creation is the result of a single creator, can there be other creators who have created other worlds that contain other forms of life and those lie beyond the domain of our creator?

If that is the case, this is something beyond the domain within which this imaginable nature exists that binds your duality to a singularity and should not theoretically concern you.

So, if your XYZ123 is a singularity and is also the owner and operator of this solo nature, we have no problem.

If there is another creator outside of this solo nature and has its own domain that never interacts at any visible or theoretical level with ours, all those other gods can be safely ignored.

The second situation where the loop of duality would not close is the more popular one. What if there are multiple creators within this solo nature?

This variant of the loop of duality can be understood better by first thinking about where XYZ123 should live.

Where to live

Where should a God live?

Experiment A   The One and Only

Where do you live? A home hopefully if you are fortunate.

What would happen if your XYZ123 decided to live amongst you?

If you want a single all-powerful Creator to be eventually titled as God, you must imagine him living beyond this world of yours. Why?

Because the trouble with more than one God existing within this solo nature can be imagined in multiple ways.

For instance, if your creators are equal co-creators, the loop of duality has not closed. Whenever you have two of anything, including gods, you have the option to choose.

If that option to choose exists within the limits of your imagination as a human, you will be able to judge between two gods of similar status.

Given that the very definition of a Creator assumes an identity beyond our natural imaginary limits, simply for god to be able to create imagination itself, the basis of our choice between any two imaginable gods will always be flawed.

Humans can, by definition, never have any power greater than a perceived creator and without the ability to have any power greater than god; we can never have any impartial basis to declare anyone as god, who can potentially create humans, let alone two.

Hence the premise of co creation by equal gods invalidates every premise that needs to be satisfied for a human to call another entity God.

This system does not provide the singularity humans desire, does not provide any viable method for humans to judge the validity of one god over another and creates one more issue.

Where will these two gods live?

If both these gods claim human to be their exclusive creation, that claim must be settled somewhere, right?

One option, which I highly recommend, is to have a Western movie style standoff on the day of judgement, where all dead and subsequently arisen humans fill a giant stadium as the two co-creators have an ultimate fight to finally show which one is the more powerful one.

The other option could be that these gods decide to live amongst us and try to get us humans to decide about their goodness so that we vote for them on the day of judgment. Kind of like the modern system of democracy where a human vote of confidence declares the victory to one divine candidate or the other.

If both candidates for God are good guys, humans should not be worried as they will simply promote their agenda positively. However, if one of the candidates is a bit naughty, it would begin to alter our choice in one way or another.

In this situation, the world as we humans know it, would become the battleground of gods. The value of a human would be nothing more than a tool of war.

In any case when we imagine two gods, the only natural question that can be raised by any other entity within the solo nature is: which one?

And the only way to solve this problem would be the elimination of one god to leave us with the ultimate singularity.

The alternate to multiple equal creators would be multiple hierarchal based system of many creators. However, that hierarchy must also terminate with a singularity at its peak or else it will suffer from the same fate as any other theory that does not assume a singularity.

These multiple creator theories also destroy the natural system within which we imagine humans having complete freedom to choose.

Therefore, if your God is indeed a singularity, it should not interact with humans below your granted level of choice, in the universe, as you know it.

Perhaps it might be best if your God XYZ123 is kept away from this human domain so that human choice is not affected.

Finally, if you wish your chosen God to indeed be all-powerful and an ultimate Singularity, it must have complete control to deliver all your desires.

Experiment A   The One and Only
_____

Just for you to be thankful to a God for a simple ice cream, your God must indeed be provided control over strawberries, ice, milk, and sugar. Without your God having ultimate control over each of these ingredients, the supply chain is at risk.

If there is another co-creator or sub-creator god within our nature who has control over cows or the clouds, those gods can potentially affect the supply of any one of the ingredients needed for ice cream.

In this model, if you were indeed to be blessed with an ice cream and wanted to thank some higher power, would you want that higher power to also be thankful to some other smaller power because it allowed cows to produce milk or did not cover the sky with clouds to kill off all strawberries?

That again would generate a version of the loop of duality which we are trying to close so that we can complete our equation of everything in nature.

Humans are already in the first dependent group that desires, and we do not want to place our Singularity within this category of dependents.

Besides, we are having trouble confirming one Singularity beyond our imagination. It would perhaps have been easier if the Singularity decided to show its face to us and when no other creator could do the same, we will finally realise that there must be only One.

Experiment A The One and Only

Revealing Face vs Attribute

If there is only One, why doesn't He just show up and put us all at peace?

Simply because, it would eliminate your choice.

Remember XYZ123 is the singularity, the only singularity and the all-powerful entity that must control every level of material and non-physical existence to ensure that your desires can be fulfilled without interruption from any other equal entity.

If XYZ123 one day, pranked you and showed up to have dinner with you, you would be left with no choice but to acknowledge XYZ123 as the ultimate Creator.

Experiment A											The One and Only

If, after this dinner, you still wanted to live, your choice must continue to exist as well. And since you would still have the choice, you could nevertheless again deny XYZ123, because He gave you that choice in the first place anyway. It would be natural for XYZ123 to take away your choice now, because after meeting Him, you still did not choose Him and wanted to meet the next candidate with similar powers.

This is the reason that your XYZ123 will never show His face to you.

If you were to imagine any singularity other than XYZ123, after dining with Him, you would need to exit this nature, restart the loop of duality, jump onto another god's domain, and find some other Creator in another system.

That seems too much work, especially given how much trouble we are having to rethink

| Experiment A | The One and Only |

everything just to confirm a single singularity within our nature. If you ever succeed in finding not one, but two singularities, let me know and I will delete this experiment.

Now if XYZ123 is not to show His face, how would you want Him to confirm its existence to you?

Would it help if instead of face, XYZ123 started to inform you of His qualities or attributes?

Take the simple example of my favorite breakfast, ice cream again. If XYZ123 declares that He is the One that created you, the cows, the clouds, the strawberries, the water, the process, the recipe, the intelligence, the labor, the factory, the fuel for delivery trucks and the other hundreds of things needed for this one simple desire plus He has control over each and every one of these elements at all times plus he also created the whole nature, within which all of the above systems operate to ensure that every time that you want ice cream, it is there for you.

Will you acknowledge that you must be thankful to just XYZ123 for fulfilling this single desire?

Instead of answering that question, try to imagine the various qualities attributable to all those involved that are needed to fulfill that single desire for ice cream. For you to say thanks to XYZ123, you would also have to confirm that the ownership of all those qualities must also lie with XYZ123. Why?

These qualities are going to be the only verifiable attributes that are available to you to acknowledge the existence of any Singularity and not a face.

Experiment A									The One and Only

Now we are getting technical and boring so it will be better to stop projecting human attributes to Singularity and let us go on something fun, like let XYZ123 create a human.

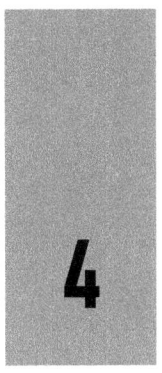

4 The Time of Creation

Do you want XYZ123 to create humans?

After all, XYZ123 is the singularity and has the option to create whatever. Your existence is known to you, and your choice confirms your duality, which is evident in this human and being combination, within which the creation of human attributes is unexplained.

To explain these attributes, you are assuming a Singularity hypothetically named XYZ123 for now. This relationship must be joined in nature for us to proceed our experiment. For now, we are calling this the relationship of Creator and Creation.

That Singularity, named XYZ123, also claims to be the Creator of this nature that hosts you.

Experiment A — The Time of Creation

If XYZ123 did indeed create humans at some point, how many?

One or Two

As you know by now, I am a human being with the sharpest memory. This exceptional quality of mine allows me to remember every ice cream I had since last week. Is your memory sharper?

How far back can you remember? Most of us can technically recall hazy details back to our earliest childhood years and that is the human limit. Memory does not transfer from one generation to another, which would have been nice as it would have allowed for all of us to remember the time of the birth (or creation) of whoever was the first human being.

Once humans gained the ability to speak and

write, we started to transfer what we thought were important details about nature and other useful knowledge so that the next generations could benefit.

Unfortunately, as I was not around when the first human was created, I could not pass on this brilliant idea of writing everything down from day one of the human creation. Therefore, we must rely on imagination.

If you imagine that one fine day XYZ123 decides to create human beings, the first question would be how many?

Apparently two. Why?

Well, I don't know but I can guess. Remember

that so far in this experiment, all that we have been able to confirm, is your existence and the existence of your choice and that is all.

That count is two already. Even if XYZ123 creates one human, it must contain a duality within for XYZ123 to be eventually acknowledged as a Singularity.

This relation of Singularity versus duality implies division.

That division must also exist at each functional level of a human being, both in the physical and the metaphysical existence.

Experiment A | The Time of Creation

If XYZ123 were to create a single human being, give it the choice, teleport that human being in this world and disappear from that human being's vision forever, what would be the grandest claim that single human being can choose to make?

I am the singularity.

That is correct. Because that single human being will have that choice.

For the very first, single unified human being who does not have any prior passed on knowledge, no one else around like him and cannot see XYZ123, drawing such a conclusion that either he is the singularity or just a fluke, after observing every other natural being on this earth, is a reasonable conclusion.

Experiment A — The Time of Creation

As we can imagine, this conclusion would be unnatural. Therefore, to eliminate this possibility that any human can unnaturally conclude that he is not subject to duality, the simplest way would be to create two at the start.

That way, all the future human beings would simply have to look at the opposite gender to conclude that division or duality, exists at every level and hence human existence can never claim Singularity. Another benefit of this system would be that it removes the presumption of intelligence for human beings to start acknowledging their own duality and start searching for a Singularity.

So, would you advise XYZ123 to create one human being or two?

The Problem of Two

What is the first problem that we face with two numbers?

Are they equal, different, or hierarchical? That is correct. This would be the first issue as soon as a human is created who is essentially a combination of dualities at each of its operational levels, including the obvious physical division.

Apparently at this moment of creation this physical division principle necessitated the creation of two human beings. As they both are creations of XYZ123, let us label one X and the other Y.

Experiment A   **The Time of Creation**

The identification of each of the two and for all those that might follow begins at this point of creation, but it now poses the first problem stated earlier. How will these two be related?

Are X and Y equal, different or in a relation of hierarchy? What would you want?

On the assumption that you imagine yourself as someone who does not have the powers of both X and Y, you belong to one of these identities.

Now you are imagining how you would place them in a formal relation, and you can have any number of arguments to support any of the three possibilities.

However, to solve this problem from the

perspective of XYZ123, you would probably consider the following:

1. Does XYZ123 want to have more humans on this earth?

2. If so, how does He sub lease this power of creation to X and Y?

If your XYZ123 decides to have more humans than two, you will have two possibilities for the creation of more humans:

First would be the same as before, where XYZ123 creates a human being personally and teleports it to earth.

The second option would be to grant the process of creation of other human beings to the two humans, X and Y. This is the same right that is given to all other non-human beings, that are sharing this earth with you.

Experiment A   The Time of Creation

By granting this ability of creation of further humans to X and Y, there will be a problem. As we established in the previous experiment F, human beings have a physical existence of being and the transcendent existence called human.

It is this transcendence of the human within this human being combination, which differentiates it from all the other beings as it contains some attributes that are not available to other beings. If XYZ123 is to be confirmed as the creator of everything including both the human and being, that human portion must both enter and exit the being to make it transcendent.

This process of the creation of the human being determines the attributes that are transferred from one human to the next.

Should these attributes be freely allowed to be transferred, or should the Original X and Y be allowed to limit this transfer to only those attribute that they have personally used, when passing them on to the future X and Y?

The introduction of this limit on the human attributes in any human after the original X and Y will give birth to another paradox.

If the attributes contained within a subsequent X or Y human being are limited to its own X and Y parent combination, this would justify the inability of any subsequent human to benefit from any human attribute contained within the original X and Y.

All attributes contained within a single human existence are never used completely, contemporaneously and to their maximum potential due to the limitation of the physical

Experiment A   The Time of Creation

---

being, as well as the ceiling of imagination.

Now if XYZ123 wants us to discover a singularity beyond imagination, using one or more of these human attributes, the existence of these human attributes must be guaranteed to all humans.

Their use is left to the human choice, and there must be several of those attributes available to a human at each time to cater for all sort of various people that inhabit this earth.

Therefore, XYZ123 must ensure that are a few attributes that are always contained in you, which when chosen to be used, should have the ability to answer some simple questions.

This core ability differentiates between human

and other beings. If you were provided with the choice whether you wish to pass on these attributes to the ones coming after you, what would happen?

You may or may not choose to pass on some attributes and if you decide not to pass on some or all the human attributes to the next humans, this decision is made by an existence that is inherently a duality and prone to error. It can also falsely identify you as the creator, as well as limiting the next human.

That is why any human, X or Y, should not be provided with this choice and XYZ123 must continue to protect and retain the copyrights to all human attributes for all future humans to maintain the singularity model Creator status.

Got bored again?

Experiment A   The Time of Creation

If yes, you are a human in need of ice cream or any other healthy mouthful you desire to exercise your jaw to ease the pressure on the brain, or any other part of your anatomy, where you think from.

If no, you have this attribute of free thought, copyrighted to XYZ123, provided to the original X and Y, transmitted from them unknowingly, preserved through all the generations, not used by some of them and yet somehow that attribute survived thousands of years, only for you to not get bored by mental exercise that you chose yourself.

Do you want to take it away for all that will follow?

If you feel like you should not have the power to take, modify or remove human attributes from any other human, even if you made one yourself, that would be a natural choice. Stealing copyrighted material off XYZ123 seems a bit risky at this stage, doesn't it?

Although to be fair, XYZ123 should also not grant humans the ability to dictate the specification of the being as well. That is irrelevant for this experiment as we are only dealing with human parts. Besides, I know if we had the choice, all of us would look young, handsome, and beautiful, just like me.

Hierarchy, Equality or Differentiation

Now at this point in the experiment, we have observed that a two human system of X and Y with both combined, having the option to create more humans without the ability to modify the

Experiment A — The Time of Creation

human portion of the created human beings is the simplest way to avoid a lot of structural top-level complexities.

In our experimental world, all knowns, so far are these:
1. You exist, as part of the people group, human or not, X or Y, but

2. You have a choice.

3. Confirmation of your human existence has already magnified the duality contained within.

4. All the above exists in a nature and for us to see everything in nature, we must search of something without a duality, that I call God, and you know as XYZ123, who has allegedly claimed that he is the sole Creator of the original X and Y.

So, is X the same as Y?

Experiment A   The Time of Creation

XYZ123 must define the relation between the two. Our options started with similarity.

Are people made like ice cream? If you visit the ice cream factory you will see that it has a highly mechanized process with precision cuts that create millions of the same ice cream cones or cups that you have had ever since you were a child, and they all look and taste the same.

Ice cream is made of a few ingredients and if our factory is fitted with atomic level precise machines, it can produce the same ice cream and prove it under the electronic microscope. We humans have created billions.

This is the concept of similarity which leads us to the definition of equality. Should XYZ123

Experiment A | The Time of Creation

create X and Y like ice creams, precisely the same?

The answer to this should depend on whether both X and Y are supposed to do similar things or not. If both are expected to take part in all human activities on this earth in an exact and equal manner as a principle, X and Y should indeed be similar in all forms.

Now XYZ123 needs to determine if this principle of similarity is suitable for humans or not. Since XYZ123 has decided to have more than one set of X and Y, this ability to produce must now be provided to both X and Y, if they are similar.

Should this principle of similarity be applied and both X and Y can produce as many more humans independently, they would not require each other.

What would happen if X and Y are similar in each way and do not require the other?

Loss of collective wisdom.

That is the real loss to all humanity combined if every human is similar, the exact copy of everyone else.

Why do we need collective wisdom?

To cut a long story short, why are you reading this?

| Experiment A | The Time of Creation |

You see. You instantly recognized that at this moment in time, you are fulfilling one of your desires, even if you are probably not enjoying it. And the greatest desire for all humankind combined is to locate at least one that does not desire.

Evidently, the task of searching for a singularity is not one person's job.

Besides if all X and all Y are the same as each other and like all other X and Y before them and none of them require anyone else as their needs, their desires, their abilities, attributes are all the same, it would limit whatever can be achieved by humanity. One replica after another, billions of times over, until the end of time.

Let me admit a deep secret buried within. Even I do not like the same ice cream for more than a few months at a time. So, are you happy with XYZ123 discarding the principle of similarity?

If yes, great, we now have a choice existing not just within us, but with the type of being who carries the human in the shape of either an X or a Y.

Now if XYZ123 wants to create this differential between X and Y, should it make the difference visible in the being as well as invisible in the human?

To be honest, I am glad that XYZ123 decided to make a quite noticeable difference between X and Y. The difference in being does not require a deep analysis to be acknowledged.

As X and Y have been granted the ability to create and contain a physical difference, how would the creation process work?

Experiment A The Time of Creation

The being of the human is pretty much like the being of other earth-based animals. The being is essentially a perfected skeletal core designed specifically to host the human, who contains certain attributes, which cannot be handled by other beings that we see around us.

XYZ123 must therefore ensure prior to the time of creation that this frame or alternate frames are tested to ensure that they do indeed contain the ability to host a human. Rigorous quality control test reports must suggest that this current skeletal frame that we call the body, or being, is the ideal vessel for the human to enter and exit and thereby becoming the most suitable form for the only transcendent reality that you have thus far discovered in the two experiments combined.

These frames are expensive however, and like all other frames of all other beings, they take time

Experiment A · The Time of Creation

to build. Should both X and Y be made responsible for building the being of the next human?

This is where the principle of similarity is formally discarded as both X and Y cannot be burdened with the very first task in the same manner.

Therefore, this task of creating another being should be assigned to either one. The agreement of both X and Y beforehand should also be made a requirement. Let us assume that Y is assigned with this exclusive task of completing the process of the creation of further humans.

Which makes me jealous of Y. The process of carrying a fetus over the term is the human replication of the natural love, possession, ownership, care and such similar attributes that can be projected onto XYZ123 at the time He

Experiment A | The Time of Creation

created the original X and Y.

Hey, wait a minute. Now that the principle of similarity has been discarded and Y has been burdened with micro x and micro y creation as a task, this seems unjust. That is why an equal responsibility needs to be assigned to X. What should that be?

That responsibility is maintenance.

Now to make the two responsibilities equal, XYZ123 must also clarify a few aspects of maintenance to satisfy the two parts of equation. How hard is production of another human being for Y?

Like the production system perfected for all

other beings, the production of humans also requires a long commitment and as part of this process, Y is also subjected to immense physical strain. As the human and being portions are combined, once that being is stretched to its physical limits over time, the human part of the human being cannot be expected to maintain all or most of its human attributes. Remember, human choice only applies up to a certain physical threshold.

Accordingly, if Y is required to undertake this assignment of production, which manifests in situations where the human attributes will vary immensely, Y must also be provided with certain assurances like acceptability for such deviations, as it is tasked with this important divine assignment. However, X is the one that must always maintain all human attributes.

This maintenance responsibility of X ought to ensure that all the natural requirements, as XYZ123 might ordain upon humans later, always continue intact permanently. Do you think that now, these two responsibilities of production and maintenance are balanced?

If yes, we have moved on from discarding the principle of similarity at the time of creation and extended the division between X and Y towards equality.

However, should you feel that this is not the case and there are other primary divisions between X and Y that are far more important, they must also be distributed in this manner to ensure balance.

To discard the principle of equality, XYZ123 would need to introduce the concept of hierarchy. In a simple system of hierarchy, XYZ123 would need to state that Y or X is of a higher status than the other and thus possesses superiority.

Experiment A   The Time of Creation

Would you want the two humans to be placed in a hierarchical system?

If yes, how would XYZ123 establish it between the first two humans, the original X and Y?

This would require XYZ123 to create one before the other. This would be the only way to ensure that in all visible and verifiable ways, X or Y could claim that superiority.

Additionally, if a hierarchical system is to be implemented, one human would need to be granted some power over the other. Neither X nor Y, are the creator of other and hence cannot claim any right over the exercise of any of the human attributes of the other. If XYZ123 is to remain the solo Creator within this nature, the

concept that X also has the right to modify humanity of Y must be unnatural.
Given that the hierarchal system is deemed unnatural, all we are therefore left with, is differentiation between X and Y on the principle of equality.

5   The Creation of Many

What would happen when X and Y are allowed to produce more humans?

There will be many. Billions of us, you, me and every person that you have ever met. So now what?

As XYZ123 has thus far maintained the copyrights to all human attributes and not allowed either X or Y to modify or remove any of these through this process of creation of billions, should XYZ123 state that it is still, the sole Creator of all the people?

Well, yes, of course. We have not needed any other entity to get to the billions in numbers and neither have all the previous generations combined been able to add or remove anything

from the human part of the human and being, this seems to be an obvious natural conclusion.
For each one in this combined humankind, duality, desire and dependence remain common which when put together continues our search for a Singularity.

However, with billions of humans for XYZ123 to claim as its creation, is there a need for all of us to maintain a separate identity?

Assignment of Identity

Who are you?

I had asked this simple question in the first experiment as well. At that time, I had allowed you to use any title to describe yourself. Whatever title you would have chosen would have probably contained a physical manifestation that would cease with the ending of your being.

Unless you said I am a human or Free bird 2000.

XYZ123 claims to have created humans and that is who we are dealing with here. If we are just human and there are billions of us and XYZ123 claims to be the sole Creator of all of us as individuals, how do we identify one from another?

In a physical sense, we are all different. Apparently, billions of us have inhabited this flat earth over thousands of years and yet, no two have been alike.

Experiment A   The Creation of Many

The being that each of our human resides in has individuality. Our faces, colour, bodies and speech are different. Even when humans are identical twins, the fingerprints are different. Our beings are not produced like ice cream cones.

This difference in physical beings is of course necessary to maintain a functional world. The simple question here is that if this difference is obvious in the physical being, does it also exist in our human parts?

If yes, we cannot see the human part of us, so how do we know it for sure?

That difference becomes apparent when human attributes are compared.

Inevitable Differentiation

Did you ever imagine yourself going through an experiment which made you imitate God?
If yes, you are in group 1, If no, group 2.

Do you intend to finish this book?

If yes, group 1A, if no group 1B.

What are we doing? We are simply taking one trait, which is free thought and sorting out the people in groups who have it.

Many people do not have this trait. Group 3.

When it comes to the meta-physical attributes of humans, the differences are limitless. Differences in beings can be limiting as most human can only have between 0 to 5 eyes for instance and not anymore.

However, when it comes to any single non-physical attribute, there are no limits.

Take intelligence for example. I have two of them. The greatest of scientists studying intelligence are unable to agree on what intelligence is.

If you study, which you are not allowed as part of this experiment, you will find out that the famous human intelligence measure IQ can only capture four kinds of intellect and that too inaccurately. Some studies identify nine, and some 12, different types of intelligence and all say there are more kinds and that most of them cannot be compared between any two people.

And this is just one of the hundreds of human non-physical attributes contained within you and me. Faith, emotions, expression, compassion and so on and so forth.

What are the odds that any one of your human attributes is the same as mine? Virtually none.

Can I find out what that human identity of yours is? Well No. Why?

I cannot see your human attributes. Neither did I create those, nor can I claim to know all hundreds of them. They are just yours because if you were also created, those were assigned to your human exclusively and most of them are protected from my manipulation.

If XYZ123 created those attributes, assigned them to you only, they define you, they remain the inevitable differentiation between all humans that have ever lived.

Given that there are always hundreds of such attributes within you, you will always remain unique.

Your individual human identity, will consequentially, only remain identifiable to XYZ123.

Freedom

Did you notice that it has been an unnaturally long time since I mentioned ice cream, and it is nearly lunch time?

If you were to examine this fact of my life, you can break it down to its sources yourself.

For instance, the hunger part is common to all beings. Do you get hungry? Of course, every being does for as long as they are alive.

Fun fact:

You can only stay alive as long as you continue to kill. It could be an animal or a plant, but it must contain live nutrients. As a side experiment for a few months, try to eat things that have never previously been alive and not killed for the momentary joy of your mouth and see if your human likes it.

Now you are free to imagine me as the killer of

ripe strawberries because I am hungry and need to make an ice cream myself. You are free to make that choice.

Furthermore, the timing of my hunger mentioned in the first statement could also differ between all people, but it is nevertheless present in all beings.

However, having ice cream for breakfast, lunch, dinner and desert for years at a time is my human choice.

You imagined me as a murderer of strawberries just a while ago because your human chose to. We established earlier in the experiment that no human can be given the power to take away all human choices from any other as a principle.

Therefore, you can continue thinking whatever about me while I continue to eat whatever I want. Again, this is the un-stealable right of choice guaranteed to all humans and some form of this right must remain within us or else our human will have no purpose left.

Can you inform me how long your being will last?

Can you know when your human will exit this being?

The answer to the first question is that you and I do not know how long our physical body will last. An invisible unknown virus could suddenly enter it through any of its openings and start to convert our own cells against us. All the doctor has to say is, "I never saw that before," and that would be the beginning of the end of our being. It could even be more sudden than that.

Experiment A — The Creation of Many

As for the timing of the human to exit this being, XYZ123 has the first natural right to decide that as He is the sole Creator and the Singularity. You are the one waiting for an appointment with any singularity that could complete your equation about everything in nature.

Would you want XYZ123 to grant that right to exit the human within, to all X and Y?

If no, this will provide you the right to complain to XYZ123, should you be unable to find a purpose in life. It will be a form of creationary slavery.

If yes, XYZ123 would have granted you the highest level of freedom that you can exercise.

The ultimate right to freely end what you can never create yourself, a human.

On the surface, allowing the humans to cease their existence seems to be an infringement upon the copyrights of XYZ123, who is the Creator of this nature as well, being a singularity, you know.

If XYZ123 did indeed provide you the power to exercise that ultimate freedom as part of your human, why?

Simply to avoid slavery. If XYZ123 is indeed the real Creator and the sole singularity, He was the one that had the option to create you without this freedom, but He chose not to make you, His slave.

If XYZ123 is confident that you already have more than enough attributes always present within you, which when applied properly, can allow you to complete the equation of nature yourself, He would also have to allow you the ultimate right to break free from your human being existence.

This way you can choose to exercise your freedom in any manner that you desire, including denial of the singularity option as well. You are not a slave and have the freedom to choose the continuity of your existence and from this moment onwards, your choices are exclusively yours with no compulsion at all from any X, Y, or XYZ123.

This is why it is also important that all X and all Y are not to be burdened with what some other X or Y chose for themselves.

Seems like a good idea to me. What about you?

Would you like to carry the burden of anyone else's choices in addition of your own's?

Imagination

"Freedom is to choose what you cannot imagine." This is a globally famous quote that most of us have been aware of since childhood. Well, no, because I just made it up. You did not know that, and it seemed like a good collection of words when put in a sentence.

The key question for you to ponder is whether you are free to imagine everything there is?

We have just seen how much freedom each human has been granted. Not only are you filled with hundreds of unique attributes, but you are also free from the burden of every other person's choice, have this ability to exercise choice to fulfill your desires that cannot be stolen, and are even free to end this contract of human being existence.

But we still have not had any confirmation that a singularity exists. All we have done thus far is to assume a singularity named XYZ123 and tried to design some natural parameters within which our existing knowledge can be vetted or explained.

But If you have all this freedom, why can't you freely imagine everything there is in our equation?

Everything in nature = Beings that desire + Anything that does not.

It would have been nice if XYZ123 did indeed have that dinner with us so we could at least put one face on the other side of the equation after the plus but that is not likely to happen.

Therefore, we are now going to need to use our imagination to explore what possible ways for a confirmation of anyone's existence after that plus could be.

How does your imagination work?

First up, you know that human brain is limited, right?

I mean can you sit at an insurance seminar and

Experiment A | The Creation of Many

not have your brain leak out of your ears? Or, even worse, having to listen to some top notch super brainiac scholar speak like this for hours:

"The ontological quintessence of consciousness, construed as a complex amalgamation of multifaceted neural architectures, inexorably interfaces with the arcane inquiry into the determinative or indeterminate substrata of the cosmos. The conceptual scaffold of volitional agency, therefore, precariously perches within the stochastic interstices delineated by the non-localized perturbations of a quantum-mechanically orchestrated reality. In addition, the hyperdimensional scaffolding underpinning the cosmic framework suggests that the intricacies of mental phenomenology may indeed be a derivative function of emergent meta-stable quantum states."

Zzzz……. Oh, sorry I fell asleep.

Experiment A	The Creation of Many

Well maybe you can. However, as XYZ123 is dealing with all humans and that also includes me, which confirms that there is a limit to the human brain and understanding.

Furthermore, there is the limit of knowledge, intellect, time to consider in addition to the natural mental limitations.

XYZ123 needs to design a system where everyone can imagine without all these limitations. What would that be?

Can you imagine a picture? Can you imagine a feeling, a sound, a thought, a dance, a ritual?

There are various ways that people imagine. The problem arises when you are asked to communicate your knowledge. Remember if all you can communicate is through a rain dance, all that is needed to break off the process of collective wisdom is one generation that has no legs.

That is why transmissible imagination, that can add to this collective wisdom to help humanity continue its search for a singularity, can only exist in the shape of a word.

Words are easy to remember: most people use them; they can be documented and are impartial; and can survive through generations either in retained memory or in written form.

If we are provided with the freedom to imagine everything, XYZ123 would probably use words as the tools through which his existence can manifest in this human world.

Experiment A   The Creation of Many
_____

So, do you want XYZ123 to talk to you?

6 The Method of Speech

That is a big question, isn't it.

Does XYZ123 need to speak to X and Y after creating them?

Remember, XYZ123 cannot show His face to you, and we are searching for someone that is not in the first part of the equation about everything in nature. The only proof of any such existence thus far has not been a face but the story of creation, which is a concept that has been passed on to you through some X or Y.

And when we look at all the transmissible intelligence of all the X and Y combined, we are informed that their collective wisdom states that there are many ways to prove or disprove the singularity using other attributes, not just words.

A lot of them would be right, indeed. As we are aware of many human attributes and there are hundreds of them, XYZ123 needs to decide something.

Should XYZ123 allow X and Y the ability to accept or deny His existence using any of the other human attributes, as He claims to be the Creator of all human attributes?

If speech, language, or words specifically were to be the only human attribute to search for a singularity, there will be a problem. Using this attribute requires physical organs, and imperfection in the beings of future X and Y could limit their search for Singularity.

Therefore, X and Y have been granted many copyrighted attributes and you have been given this natural ability to search for a Singularity yourself using any combination of them.

You can use this natural ability to come up with any answer about Singularity and it will likely be, naturally correct.

However, when you try to use your own method for confirmation or denial of the Singularity and attempt to pass it on to another X or Y, the natural variation in individual attributes will not allow perfection in transmission of the collective wisdom.

Therefore, if your proof requires any attribute that is not impartial, it can be questioned, as it was passed on by some X or Y to you and you passed on others.

Which human attribute makes you understand the most, has the greatest capacity to store collective wisdom, and is impartial?

Language. That is correct.

Hence, we come to the concept of language before we get to the word part of speech.

So when should XYZ123 start speaking?

Experiment A • The Method of Speech

The Start

What should be the first words that you would want XYZ123 to say to the first X and Y?

Ice cream? Seems like a reasonable choice to me. I mean it is yummy, nice, cold and sweet, and is a complete and healthy meal.

Although, I wonder that if ice cream is injected inside your veins, it could be deadly, perhaps. I don't know.

If the Original X and Y did indeed find ice cream and intravenous needles on day one of creation, they will not know this either.

Unless XYZ123 also decided that He must teach this newly created creation, the idea of a duality.

Do this. Don't do that. You know, choice.

This will require language. A key purpose of all language has been the capturing of as much information as our limited brain can store to kickstart the process of collective wisdom using the human attribute of intelligence.

Which language did XYZ123 use to speak of the Original X and Y?

Again, I don't know. I am a flawed human myself with a limited brain just like you. And I am so dumb that I thought ice cream would be a great

Experiment A   The Method of Speech

---

word for XYZ123 to start the language.

Anyway, if you are still alive and still thinking, it is probably in some language, that I may or may not know, but language is one of humanity's truest impartial attribute.

Once some X and Y gained the ability to document language, we started the transmission of information. And much of this transmitted language from all previous X and Y has been documented.

That was the beginning of the accumulation of information, which all subsequent X and Y have used to produce wisdom, the collective lesson of which has been that there must be some XYZ123, statistically.

The proof of this lies in searching for the number of people that believe in One God, like me, and call themselves human.

As you still have the choice to say no, do we have any documented proof somewhere that the Original X and Y indeed were provided with this information using one of their human attributes in some form, that allowed X not to inject Y with intravenous needle with flowing ice cream?

Meaning, did XYZ123 provide the natural ability to Original X and Y, to tell the right thing from wrong?

The answer to this question is going to need an impartial proof, you know a word.

Experiment A   The Method of Speech

To create a word in any language, you need some things like paper and pen, and idea and time, and the realisation that it is important, and all arrangement for this writing experiment is going to take time.

XYZ123 after having provided the natural ability to original X and Y, must now allow time to pass for there to be as many more X and Y that are needed to create written language. During this time, He might have had an ice cream, who knows?

I just realised I am hungry. I suggest you too go and eat something. In our experimental world, some early X and Y have started writing information for you to come back and process it into wisdom.

The End
Where were we?

Ahh…. I just remembered we ate! Whatever formerly alive plant or animal was sacrificed and forcibly made part of your protoplasmic being was supposedly created by some XYZ123, who also created the human part that is reading this.

And as per collective wisdom, we are presented with this idea that XYZ123 must also have spoken to the original X and Y, who told their kids who were probably concentrating on their ice cream and not paying full attention. Who knows?

Experiment A — The Method of Speech

To remove the jokes from some serious information, some early X and Y also created the ability to write, which eventually evolved as an impersonal and impartial yardstick of wisdom, since everyone used the same medium to add their own knowledge to it.

Which presented us with a problem. All words ever, have been written by either an X or Y, both of whom are mortal humans, containers of duality in every sense of the word.

We need a system to know which words can trustworthily be identified as having been sourced from XYZ123 and which have been added by some other X or Y, now that there are millions of these dualities who can all also write.

What could that system be?

Experiment A							The Method of Speech

Before creating a system of validation of words and its sources, we need to recall the massive variation in all the human attributes.

If XYZ123 used the human attribute of language to communicate the initial information on safety, responsibility, purpose, identity and ice cream recipe to the original X and Y, some of this information would not have been properly passed on to the forthcoming X and Y generations.

Due to freedom of choice, variation of attributes and a lack of an impartial, impersonal permanent system of writing to store collective wisdom, many additions to the original words are inevitable.

Experiment A   The Method of Speech

In a nature, where all words are equal and can be rightfully questioned by anyone, singularity cannot exist.

If XYZ123 needs to maintain its Creator status, He must inform some X which words He owns, and which were added. It must be an X, if you agree that responsibility of maintenance is X's job.

From here on, begins all form of faith, where beliefs are developed using divine words communicated to an X or Y, and the idea that all words that we use can also can now be divided into their divine or human origin.

XYZ123 has already communicated with 3 humans. The original X and Y and the One that was chosen to identify natural form unnatural words once this ability to write was developed.

There might have been more, but we are only designing this experimental world to find out the bare minimum realities that can make this nature operate the way it is.

If XYZ123 does indeed choose to speak to some X and Y, we can start arranging words in divine or human buckets and now, we have a hierarchy of words.

These 'holy' words are not just the representative of collective wisdom but have also been certified by some chosen humans as belonging to XYZ123, should you choose faith.

Should XYZ123 cease this option of personally speaking to X and Y to stop this certification of words?

In other words, do you want XYZ123 to stop speaking to all X and Y?

The Why

XYZ123 whispered to the original X and Y, and He also spoke to One (or maybe more) to ensure that certain pages of His words exist too as documentary proof, thereby adding the stamp of His approval on some words that became famous as holy.

Do we need XYZ123 to keep stamping His approval to make more holy words? It depends.

Why do you think we need more holy words? What else is left for us to question?

Experiment A   The Method of Speech

What is the grandest unsolved problem left within any person that has not been answered inside the meaning of all existing holy words of various kinds available currently?

Here is a nice assignment for you to do after you are done with this book. Take a piece of paper, an ice cream and a pen.

Come up with a question yourself that you need the answer of. Write it down.

If your question can be answered by any other words written by an X or Y, you were just ignorant about your question.

If your question cannot be answered by holy words, Congratulation! we have a winner.

Experiment A   The Method of Speech

One complicated question created by you that was left unanswered by XYZ123 when He spoke with the original X and Y and another One (or more) who documented it for collective wisdom.

That winning question will need an answer now.
If the answer does not exist in the 'holy' words ratified by XYZ123, you would first need to study those words before claiming that there is no answer there, and hence, you can now claim that you created a unique paradox.

After that you can use that question and source the answer from any other X or Y, but remember, in this experimental world of ours, you are alone, and you do not have other people around to source your answers from yet.

Experiment A — The Method of Speech

Hence do this assignment as a homework task.

If you do not find the answer to one original unanswered question within holy words, you will have four choices.

1. Find the answer from another X or Y.

2. Declare that there is no XYZ123 as you outsmarted that candidate for Singularity, so must now search for another candidate.

3. Say that everything in nature is just a fluke, or

4. Perhaps you need more holy words.

As I finished my forty seventh ice cream and my own paper was blank, I concluded that I, myself,

Experiment A | The Method of Speech

do not need any more holy words and there are already enough stamped by my God, so I became a human.

However, for you to conclude that you need more holy words, you would have to discard all other options, but that journey must begin with the study of the holy words themselves, which is not allowed in this experiment.

However, any X or Y can claim that they are either waiting for more holy words, or are super busy, as they all have that choice.

Meanwhile, XYZ123 also has the option to mention that this is it, no more holy words.

If an X or Y does not take the time to study the

already stamped, and in ample supply of various kinds of holy words, provided in written, printed or digital forms in many languages and since virtually forever, the newly formed paradox remains invalid ab initio.

(For my non-French speakers, ab initio means from the start in Spanish. And yes, I can translate it into many other complicated languages, but I am not trying to show off here.)

Given that our experimental world already contains the equation that can help any X or Y to see everything in nature if they participate in collective wisdom, has ample holy words and enough human attributes that can deny or confirm any Singularity, perhaps there is no harm in XYZ123 choosing His option to not speak anymore.

What do you think?

 7   The Protection of Word

Do you want XYZ123 to not speak to any X or Y from now on?

In fact, it does not matter if XYZ123 does or not. Why?

If XYZ123 is indeed still secretly speaking to some alive X or Y, how will you know? The only way for you to know that XYZ123 is still handing our fresh recipes for ice cream secretly through some selected X or Y, it will be through those 'chosen' X or Y.

Will you believe that claim from any X or Y?

Experiment A 　　　　　　　　　　　　　　　　The Protection of Word

If you choose yes, you are making that decision based on zero evidence and faith exclusively.

Remember, XYZ123 cannot show his face in this nature and if you choose to believe that some existing X or Y, another person with the same human attributes as yourself, has suddenly been granted a face-to-face meeting, or a phone call with XYZ123, that is the beginning of reliance on words of another X or Y that have not been marked holy as yet.

That is unless XYZ123 chooses to stamp these new words as 'Holy'. How does any XYZ123 stamp his approval on the words of any X or Y?

The problem that we saw with words is their possibility of misinterpretation. When I called you limited, what did it mean?

Experiment A								The Protection of Word

We already know that your brain is limited- it cannot store unlimited information; your eyes can be five at most, they can see only a short distance; your ice cream consumption is limited to thirty per meal at most, and so on and so forth.

This is called an interpretation of words- the expansion of each word to figure out what exactly is included inside that word. Your interpretation of limitedness will always differ from mine because even though we may look reasonably close replicas in our physical form, the human attributes within us are unique, which allows for various interpretations of any word ever spoken by any X or Y.

It is this variation of extracting your own meaning of each word that allows you to question anything, as part of the choice granted to you by your XYZ123.

That is the reason that XYZ123 must stamp certain words and proclaim that these are error free when combined as a principle, explanation or rule, even if all X and Y initially differ on what each of the individual words include within them.

That will be the only way that any XYZ123 can compile a list to be identified as commandments, if you want XYZ123 to also command this nature as its Creator.

Not to get very technical here, but this is exactly how all laws ever created by human work. If you do not believe me and want to get a nice long sleep, turn on any channel showing you any courtroom filled with judges and lawyers going on and on for hours to try to convince each other that the definition of reckless includes intravenously injecting ice cream after 5 pm on Friday as well.

Experiment A The Protection of Word

This is exactly why XYZ123 also needs to stamp His approval on certain words to make them holy. The same way that approval is needed to create laws of any country.

Who will stamp these words as holy?

You already know that XYZ123 Himself, is not likely to come down and do it personally. However, given that XYZ123 is not just the Creator of X and Y, but also the Singularity, XYZ123 also has the option to add anyone else to the mix, like a Z.

Hear me out here. This might be the most brilliant idea of mine that does not involve ice cream.

If all X and Y have the option to question the word of the other, there will always be doubts. The easiest way to remove these would be to say some Z (that is of a higher status than X and Y) was sent by XYZ123 to tell both X and Y which commands can be considered holy.

This is an easy fix to remove doubts. If XYZ123 chose that method, any X or Y could still claim that this Z could be a duality itself and so how will we know the true intent and origin of Z?
That is a micro variation of the loop of duality, which must be kept closed and not reopen in this experiment. Hence, we will not consider any Z and must only rely on X and Y.

We still have not solved the problem of who gets to stamp words as holy, and we only have X and Y as options?

Experiment A   The Protection of Word

Why did we need a Z though? The reason we started to imagine a Z was to claim some form of superiority for an X or Y, over all the other X and Y, so that we could create this category of holy words.

If all X and Y were created on the principle of equality, the only way to display that superiority would be for the stamp bearing X or Y to have unquestionable powers beyond what an X and Y can possess.
What could that be? Knowledge?

If you were lucky enough to meet someone that knows it all- if someone exists that can fit this description- what will happen?

Experiment A   The Protection of Word

You will be left speechless.

No unanswered questions, no ability to doubt, all answers naturally provided and understood by your human within you. That is the ideal outcome from your meeting with someone who has all the knowledge.

Does that person also possess the ability to remove your choice to believe in anything or not?

As a matter of principle, no, whoever that person might be.

Therefore, XYZ123 needs to provide the stamp bearing X or Y not just the knowledge, but also the ability to not just leave you speechless, but

Experiment A	The Protection of Word

spokenless (c) too.

XYZ123, therefore, in addition to not just selecting an X or Y, must also provide them the ability to display beyond human attributes to the chosen One (or Ones), which cannot be questioned by the combined collective wisdom of all past, present and future X and Y.

Although to be fair, you could still say, "No, I still do not believe whatever this X or Y, who may have beyond human attributes, says". XYZ123 must also provide this choice to you too as you are not a slave. So, happy with this system?

Well, that is what has been provided in the story of creation by the collective wisdom that claims a Singularity.

You are of course, free to think of an alternative.

So, think of any doubts to raise. There can be a lot, trust me.

Avoiding Human Pollution

Irrespective of whether you agreed with the system created for stamping the seal of approval on certain words by XYZ123, we have a problem:

For you to deny the existence of a Singularity, you would need to study all these holy words within this collective wisdom and come up with a list of original unanswered questions that are not

Experiment A   The Protection of Word

---

rooted in your ignorance, and this seems too much work because you know, we are lazy.

Besides, you are not allowed to read the words of another X, Y or XYZ123 as part of this experiment in any case. So, let us raise some doubts to avoid this massive post-experiment work and maintain our laziness records intact.

Let us raise doubts on the process of this so-called certification, or stamp of approval. And we can think of many ways that this can be achieved:

Did X or Y write without an error? Who knows?
Did the chosen X and Y have the time to write, proofread, edit, explain each word individually? Maybe not!

Experiment A — The Protection of Word

Was the stamp bearing X or Y asked every possible question? Certainly not!

Do human proofreaders make mistake? Yes!

Can errors or omissions happen while producing copies? Yes!

Can a book or a page be lost? Yes!

Can you spill ice cream on a paragraph? Of course!

Can the stamp bearing X or Y have an alternate motive, being a duality? Maybe!

You see, with hardly any effort, we can generate more than enough reasonable doubts. And even though the stamp bearing X or Y would have likely communicated the true original words of XYZ123, we can still doubt and question these words. And the beyond human attribute miracles can be classified as black magic.

Experiment A   The Protection of Word

That again is the exercise of the choice given to each person.

However, if you doubt holy words on any ground in the manner listed above, the following is the comprehensive list of choices that you are left with in our experimental world:

1.

That is correct.

Remember, you cannot rely on the word of any other X or Y, which includes me, or any XYZ123, which you doubt.

Experiment A 　　　　　　　　　　　　　　　　　The Protection of Word

Your journey in this experimental world where impartiality can only exist in the form of written words will cease.

If you agree with the principle that the word of any XYZ123 must be superior to the word of any X or Y, your question must be unanswered within the words spoken to you by XYZ123, or else they will just be based on ignorance.

Therefore, once you complete this experiment and exit this experimental world and go back to the real world, as you knew before and want to speak, you will have a problem.

Which words will you choose? Your choice will be either to raise a question and look for the answer within the naturally stamped holy words or raise a question and ask another X or Y with the hope that you are just ignorant.

Experiment A · The Protection of Word

For you to avoid these options as the only two choices left when you exit this experimental world, I have a suggestion for you.

Avoid human pollution.

This means that you go to the collective wisdom of humanity, wherever you think that exists, sort all words that have ever existed in two buckets, labelled Holy Words and Human Words and forget all doubts raised upon the holiness of the words within that Holy Words bucket.

I am not suggesting that you believe everything you see in this bucket of Holy Words as it will contain everything that not just XYZ123 has potentially stamped, but that bucket will also contain every other singularity claimant's words too in addition to all those other people that think a Singularity is not needed to complete the equation of everything you see in nature, and faked the stamp of approval.

However, that bucket of all words marked Holy, will be the next Experiment that you must conduct.

Without accepting them as true, how do you start sorting everything contained in that bucket?

How do you find the important bits?

What if that is too much work and you need the help of some other X or Y?

Experiment A — The Protection of Word

One final gift for the truly lazy.

Let me suggest a shortcut. Instead of sorting out that whole bucket of Holy Words, which needs a lot of time, just search for the Do's and Don'ts.

You know, look for items that ask the created human to do some simplest of things and not to do certain things because they will cause pain.

Hey X, do take care of your Y and don't inject ice cream intravenously, as it will kill you. That kind of stuff.

If you conclude after reading all such commands of XYZ123, that He does not wish to cause you harm simply for questioning anything, that would be your naturally preferred choice, right?

If you wish to be harmed by XYZ123 just to ask a question raised by one of the human attributes within you, He claims to have created, why?

Hence, the only way for you to turn to that bucket of Holy Words would be to approach it with no pollution created from other humans or your own attributes.

8 The Timeframe

How much of this is left?

Fair question and how rude! Did I bore you? Are you tired? Hungry? Sleepy?

All are very natural questions, and you have the right to ask these from me. Do you know that you also have the right to ask the same questions to XYZ123?

If you decide to ask XYZ123, "How many more ice creams do I got left?" should XYZ123 answer it?

Experiment A · The Timeframe

Again, two possibilities, yes or no. So let us examine. So, if XYZ123 did create you, in two parts, filled your human part with certain attributes not available to any other kind of beings that you see around you, allowed you to exercise complete freedom, should XYZ123 also inform of the time that this transcendent experience of yours will finish?

How?

XYZ123 cannot speak to you. You are not important enough to be specifically mentioned in all the holy words. As per the rules of this experiment, XYZ123 can in no natural way inform you of when your being will cease and your human will exit, and as we already established, that event is an inevitable, undeniable reality.

The only reality besides your existence, which you can learn about yourself, just by observing

Experiment A — The Timeframe

every other being that is alive.

You do not need any other X or Y to know about the inevitability of death. Therefore, this eventuality of the death of the being can now also be added to our experimental world as a certainty.

The only part that can be questioned is what would happen to the human following the death of its associated being. Once again, you have the availability of the story of creation to know what all combined collective wisdom says.

At the end of this experiment, you certainly have the option to find out what that story is. There is always a chance that the story provided is the one that appears natural to you.

Alternatively, you always have the option to reject it, decide XYZ123 may not be the best suited candidate for a Singularity, discard XYZ123 or rename it to any other candidate you want to adopt as your Singularity, or give up this search and declare yourself a fluke.

However, all the above requires some work. Step one would be to approach the bucket of Holy Words, sort it out and find out yourself, if you do not wish to ask any other X or Y.

Without this step one, there is no other natural conceivable manner, in which you could have any hope to even imagine seeing everything there is to see in nature.

Till that time, all you would know is yourself, a container of dualities and doubts.

Experiment A The Timeframe

But one with hope.

The hope that you have enough time on hand to sort all this out yourself before XYZ123 decides to end the experiment. Structurally, XYZ123 cannot tell you when that will happen, and you cannot pray without acknowledging XYZ123 first, so all you really have is hope.

And I do not want my God to take away my hope. What about you? Do you hope for more time?

Sorry.

As your time with me is finished, this is the end of our experiment.

Experiment A · The Timeframe

9 The End and Beyond

The End

Once again, you went through this experiment and learned absolutely no knowledge.

And I delivered what was promised, I hope.

The Beyond

Here is all we have in our experimental world:

1. You, a duality
2. Your choice of anything
3. Words, human or holy
4. Combined desire of all humanity to search for a singularity
5. Death

Experiment A

Did I miss anything in the above list?

What else is there that you have so far really known as certainty that is not listed above, in the two experiments combined?

All we have established is that you exist, have a human inside your body that is making you read this, you can choose to stop at any time, yet you continue reading even when this experiment has ended and beyond because our human continues to desire at each moment, for something.

Our bodies, of course, stop desiring for some time, once we have stuffed it with ice cream. Even when our associated being rests, our humans do not. The collective wisdom of everyone like us has been trying to tell you that

Experiment A

---

this restlessness is due to the limits of what you can know.

Every piece of knowledge you have ever gained has been the result of your desire to know more and irrespective of how many words you store inside your brain, or any other part of your anatomy, they will only add to the pile accumulated on one side of the equation about nature, because you desired it.

The greatest story of creation, that all combined humanity has agreed upon statistically, has the potential to complete that equation, should you begin dissecting the story slowly and carefully.

The natural starting point of this dissection asks you to go to the holy bucket first as it is the more important one and start looking at words and what they mean and what they tell you. Remember, for you to come up with a better story, you must know what you are competing against.

Oh…I almost forgot: Also, in none of the two buckets, lies one critical information- that of course being the time of your death.

That is all there is.

You can of course, choose to take this natural journey of discovery or indeed have yet another ice cream.

That choice is yours, and you know me, I never meddle in your personal affairs.

Experiment A

Oh, if you do decide to take the journey of discovery or the creation of the ultimate paradox that finds not one but 345 other XYZ123s, you could go alone.

Or you could take someone along, another trustworthy X or Y. Someone you can trust.

And remember when you approach that bucket of Holy Words to search for Singularity, you will need to deep dive in language, meaning of words and where they start from. Like what does XYZ123 start from?

www.ingramcontent.com/pod-product-compliance
Lightning Source LLC
Chambersburg PA
CBHW071005160426
43193CB00012B/1927